Advance Praise for *Meowku*:

Enjoy a delightful romp of word play through a New York filled with mischievous cats and kittens. Accompanied by lovely photos, Patricia Carragon's poems capture moments of city life with feline friends, and sometimes, foes. Who knew that these ancient Japanese forms fit modern New York life with cats so *purr*fectly?

— JUDY KAMILHOR, AUTHOR OF *BEFORE THE BIG BANG* AND *CAT DREAMS*

Patricia Carragon is known throughout our creative and feline worlds as "that Brooklyn girl." The humor, noblesse, and yes, loveliness of her nationwide nurturing presence are aptly, beautifully encapsulated within these thirty-five pages of photos, haiku, and micro (yet mighty) poems. *Meowku* is a nurturing "cattitude" we all need.

— AYAZ DARYL NIELSEN, EDITOR OF *BEAR CREEK REVIEW*

Praise for *Urban Haiku and More*:

Patricia Carragon hits the haiku right on the head, making it as much her form as the masters'. Funny and deadly accurate, they stop you in your tracks. It's no accident that she starts off with a Kerouac and Bashô haiku. She frees up the territory: Bashô's frogs are replaced by bedbugs; Kerouac's drugs are replaced by Viagra. Very feminine with no holds barred — very astute and timely — a great read — guaranteed to free up your notions of what a haiku can't or can do.

— HAL SIROWITZ, AUTHOR OF *STRAY CAT BLUES*, SECOND POET LAUREATE OF QUEENS, NEW YORK (2001 - 2004)

Urban Haiku and More is a fun read, with serious undertones. As with her earlier book, *Journey to the Center of My Mind* (Rogue Scholars Press, 2005), the images are sharp and pulsing. . . . The poems on these 37 pages run the gamut of observation. Love, anger, and cynicism, and the guts to say it like it is, are side-by-side with more meditative musings that turn, in what I think of as 'vintage' Carragon, into a moment of shocking reality, which can offer a more meditative read as well. . . . What might appear to be a simple little read surprises and engages us again and again. I thoroughly enjoyed *Urban Haiku and More* and think you will too.

— KAREN NEUBERG, *GENTLY READ LITERATURE*

In *Urban Haiku and More*, Patricia Carragon brings something else to the table. There's a kind of urbane wittiness to these works, by turns caustic, plaintive, engaging, and abrupt — a kimono-clad harkening to Whitman's notion of the Barbaric Yawp.

— GEORGE WALLACE, *BIG CITY LIT*

MEOWKU

CITY CALICO

MEOWKU

Poems & Photographs
Patricia Carragon

POETS WEAR PRADA • Hoboken, New Jersey

Meowku

Copyright © 2019 Patricia Carragon

All rights reserved. Except for use in any review or for educational purposes, the reproduction or utilization of this work in whole or in part in any form by electronic, mechanical or other means, now known or hereafter invented, including xerography, photocopying and recording, or in any informational or retrieval system, is forbidden without the written permission of the publisher:

>Poets Wear Prada
>533 Bloomfield Street, Second Floor
>Hoboken, New Jersey 07030
>http://pwpbooks.blogspot.com

First North American Publication 2019
First Mass Market Paperback Edition 2019

Grateful acknowledgment is made to the following publications where some of these poems originally appeared:

>*The Avocet: A Journal of Nature Poetry, Bear Creek Haiku, Clockwise Cat, First Literary Review-East,* Poetry Super Highway's *Haikuniverse, Tamarind* collation magazine, *What Happens Next* collation magazine, Local Gems Press's *13 Days of Halloween* newsletter and print anthology (2016), *Urban Haiku and More* (Fierce Grace Press, 2010), and various Brevitas anthologies (2014 - 2018), published in conjunction with the annual Brevitas Festival of the Short Poem.

ISBN-13: 978-1-946116-21-5   ISBN-10: 1-946116-21-1

Printed in the U.S.A.

Front Cover Photograph: Patricia Carragon, *Sad Eyes*
Author Photo: Marc-André Runcie-Unger

For Carmel and Callen

Cats tell me without effort all that there is to know.
— Charles Bukowski

Holding up my purring cat to the moon. I sighed.
— Jack Kerouac

The cat is the beautiful devil.
— Charles Bukowski

For he will do
As he do do
And there's no doing anything about it!
— T.S. Eliot

In the morning frost the cats step, slowly
— Jack Kerouac

Their musk clings in the entries to good ladies' houses.
— William Carlos Williams

haiku kittens
17 purrs and hisses
describe the moment

        (for Tama)
        the goddess meows
            Kishigawa's good fortune
              calico's blessings

    the maneki-neko
        waves her calico paw
           "meowzel tov"

topaz sunlight
the storefront cat
makes eye contact

      in V formation
           pigeons fly over the city
                  cat jumps off wing chair

feline companions
cat ladies anonymous
men need not apply

inspiration
    from her mews
        she scratches the page

        feline etiquette
        humans must cater to cats
        never vice versa

kitty rubs
against your legs
free massage

SLEEPING FURBALL

kitten catnaps by steps
oblivious
to noontime sun

                sleeping kittens
                on the bed
                furball quilt

        the cat falls asleep
        the dog runs to the kitchen
        the mice ate their food

hissy fit
kitty wants to be fed
NOW!

                                        faucet waterfall
                                        thinking of cats and haiku
                                        while brushing my teeth

                Kerouac kitty
                poems unravel
                like toilet paper

kitten caboodle
litter box quicksand hides poop
but not the scent

        litterary cats:
            Kindle subscribers
                in Amazon's litter box

    do cats have 9 lives
    to outwit, outsmart, outdo
    Internet junkies?

TERRITORIAL CAT

outside Brooklyn homes
    silent roars from stone lions
        March winds growl and hiss

behind iron gates
    an ornamental cat rests
        casting its shadow
            on a garden rock
                nearby houses protected
                    by concrete lions

Brooklyn felines
cattitude
comes with the territory

                          tails of tomcats
                          territorial showdown
                          Brooklyn howl

        Cheshire Cat in black
        curls up . . . disappears up close
              trash bag in disguise

GROUCHO CAT

catlike plastic bag
crosses my path
a real cat makes her presence

        tuxedo kitten
           climbs the chain-link fence
              makes that Olympian leap

    when daffodils bloom
    pregnant calicoes sashay
    down garden catwalks

by the tulip patch
a momma cat
hides her kittens

                                  outdoor litter box
                                  kittens spread fertilizer
                                  rose bushes thrive

              nocturnal love nest
              outside my building
              kitty hookers in heat

PEEKING TABBY

at midnight
feline karaoke
gets hotter

                                      backyard rumble
                                      raccoons amuse
                                      the indoor cat

              summer heat
              tell that to
              the sleeping cat

temperature rises
yowling cats by the bush
feral heatwave

                                          heatwave
                                          my train runs
                                          on cat time

              calicoes resist
              the macho tom's persistence
              ovaries on strike!

CAT ON STOOP

between two tomcats
anger management discord
midsummer mayhem

        newborn kittens killed
        blood on tomcat's mouth
        love is not for everyone

    on a blanket of leaves
    neighborhood kittens
    play hide-and-seek

Halloween night
black cats caterwaul
at the full moon

                        Halloween moonlight
                        black cats fight
                        for dominance

        ghostly calicoes
        toms the color of midnight
        catnip bewitches

eyes of the cat witch
hypnotize her devotees
cuteness wins more treats

        calico witches
              black cats fight for dominance
                    Halloween howl

     calico witches
          high on vampire catnip
               Halloween howl

CAT APPROACHING

    Frankenstein kitties
        chase calicoes on broomsticks
            Halloween howl

        Count Catcula bites
            the necks of hissing black cats
                Halloween howl

    meltdown on Bay 17th
    ghosts of cats, squirrels, and birds
    emerge from ice

the cat leaves a Christmas present
in the litter box
the scent of shit happening

                                        by the window
                                        a snowflake meltdown
                                        amuses the cat

                the cat enjoys fresh snowfall
                but the squirrel hides
                under the a/c

inside an old box
the calico seeks shelter
December snowstorm

        dinner table scraps
        trash bags ripped for survival
        hungry kittens eat

humans too busy
to notice the thirsty cat
underneath the car

the thirsty cat drinks
from a courtyard puddle
sees his reflection

                                        when the lights go out
                                        cries from the cat
                                        take over the apartment

                outside the bedroom door
                early morning meows
                give her food or else

THE INTROSPECTIVE CAT

cat-bite systems
more powerful than
computer bytes

        the mischievous cat
        curls up on the windowsill
        plans her next attack

(for Alison Ross)
progressive claws
send political machines
to the shredder

if kittens could vote
Donald Trump's wig would be sold
as kitty litter

                      keep your pussy
                      rodent free
                      kick him in the ballot!

        seeking sanity
        in the Age of Trump
        cat meditation

like cat's eyes
doors to inner space
open and shut

        the singing bowl
        cannot compete
        with the purring cat

    Savasana
    cat whiskers brushing
    the human on the mat

MORNING SHADOWS

(for Steve Luttrell)
like a cat
        the wind
                has its own agenda

                sleeping cat
                her calm
                before the storm

morning shadows
on sidewalk
a cat crosses

outside my building
yellow eyes behind bushes
nature's litter box

WEST SIDE CONDO

Acknowledgments

The author would like to thank the publishers and editors of the various publications where these poems first appeared, sometimes in a slightly different format or version:

"(for Tama) the goddess meows,"   *Bear Creek Haiku Blogspot*
"feline companions," "kitty rubs,"
"sleeping kittens," "Brooklyn felines,"
"at midnight," "inside an old box,"
"when the lights go out,"
"outside the bedroom door,"
"the mischievous cat,"
"(for Alison Ross) progressive claws,"
"like cat's eyes," "sleeping cat,"
"outside my building"

"faucet waterfall," "kitten caboodle,"   *Bear Creek Haiku* print magazine
"litterary cats,"
"outside Brooklyn homes,"
"tuxedo kitten," "by the tulip patch,"
"backyard rumble," "summer heat,"
"heatwave," "keep your pussy,"
"Savasana"

"topaz sunlight," "Kerouac kitty,"   *First Literary Review-East*
"(for Steve Luttrell) like a cat"

"Cheshire Cat in black"   Local Gems Press's *13 Days of Halloween* newsletter, October 21, 2016. (Reprinted by Local Gems Press, same year, in subsequent print anthology bearing the same name as the newsletter.)

"when daffodils bloom," "temperature rises"	*Tamarind* collation magazine, April 2013, May 2018
"eyes of the cat witch"	Poetry Super Highway's *Haikuniverse*, October 31, 2015
"behind iron gates," "the thirsty cat drinks"	*The Avocet: A Journal of Nature Poems* print journal
"ghostly calicoes," "by the window," "the cat enjoys fresh snowfall"	*The Weekly Avocet* newsletter
"if kittens could vote"	*Clockwise Cat*, Issue 34: Clockwise Rain, June 2016
"kitten catnaps by steps" (2018), "tails of tomcats" (2014), "catlike plastic bag" (2016), "on a blanket of leaves" (2017), "meltdown on Bay 17th" (2015), "seeking sanity" (2017), "the singing bowl" (2017), "morning shadows" (2018)	various Brevitas anthologies (2014 - 2018), published in conjunction with the annual Brevitas Festival of the Short Poem
"newborn kittens killed"	*What Happens Next* collation magazine, #36: Out of Order, June 2013.

The following haiku were reprinted from *Urban Haiku and More* (Fierce Grace Press, 2010):
"in V formation," "inspiration," "the cat falls asleep,"
"outdoor litter box," and "the cat leaves a Christmas present."

The author is proud to be recognized in the Living Haiku Anthology, the largest global online repository of quality published haiku from around the world, edited by Dr. Richard Gilbert, Kumamoto University, Japan: "the cat enjoys snowfall" is among the twelve haiku selected to represent her contribution to this poetic form.

Special thanks to Marc-André Runcie-Unger for the back cover photograph and for posting "outside Brooklyn homes," "tuxedo kitten," and "behind iron gates" online in Katzenworld's Purrsday Poetry (https://katzenworld.co.uk).

Also by Patricia Carragon

Journey to the Center of My Mind
New York City: Rogue Scholars Press, 2005

Urban Haiku and More
Illustrated by William L. Hays
Pooler, GA: Fierce Grace Press, 2010

Innocence
Georgetown, KY: Finishing Line Press, 2017

The Cupcake Chronicles
Hoboken, NJ: Poets Wear Prada, 2017

A NOTE ON THE TYPE

This book is set in Minion Pro, an Old-Style serif typeface designed by Robert Slimbach of Adobe Systems, and released in 1990 by Linotype. Inspired by the mass-produced publications of the late Renaissance, but with a contemporary crispness and clarity not possible with the print machinery of that era, even by the best of the Renaissance typographers, this modern-day interpretation is well regarded for its classic baroque-rooted styling and its enhanced legibility. One of the five or six most widely used typefaces for trade paperback fiction published in the United States over the past several years, Minion Pro is the typeface adopted by the Smithsonian for its logo. The name Minion is derived from the traditional classification and nomenclature of typeface sizes; minion, the size between brevier and nonpareil, approximates a modern 7-point lettering size.

www.ingramcontent.com/pod-product-compliance
Lightning Source LLC
Chambersburg PA
CBHW071802040426
42446CB00012B/2672